THE RIDGEWAY

The Ridgeway
Europe's oldest road

Richard Ingrams

Paintings from the Francis Kyle Gallery

PHAIDON · OXFORD

Phaidon Press Limited, Littlegate House, St. Ebbe's Street,
Oxford OX1 1SQ

First published 1988
© Phaidon Press Limited 1988

British Library Cataloguing in Publication Data

The Ridgeway: Europe's oldest road.
  1. Ridgeway Path (England)—Description
and travel—Views
  914.22   DA670.R5/
  ISBN 0-7148-2506-9

Printed in Great Britain by Ebenezer Baylis & Son Ltd., The Trinity Press,
Worcester and London

*The endpapers are reproduced from the Ordnance Survey of England and Wales
¼-inch map series, Sheet 19, published in 1900. Courtesy Bodleian Library, Oxford*

Page 2: Graham Hillier. From Hackpen. *Acrylic, 1986*

Contents

Foreword
The Ridgeway Exhibition

Francis Kyle

The idea of an exhibition of paintings based on the landscape of the Ridgeway came up first in conversation with my friend and fellow walking enthusiast, Philip Hughes, who pointed out how close the old track lay to modern urban developments such as Swindon — an unsuspected proximity of new and ancient. Would it not be a challenge to bring them together by arranging for contemporary artists to look in depth at the area and show their work near the landscape which inspired it?

In June 1985 I invited a group of artists to visit the Ridgeway between Avebury and the Thames at Streatley over the course of a year. The artists were selected, first, for their commitment to landscape. Several among them, including Keith Grant and Philip Hughes, were well acquainted already with their subject, but it seemed to me appropriate to establish a wider perspective on this wonderful landscape by also including artists I knew from France, Austria, Germany and the United States. One artist, Malte Sartorius, perhaps the most respected etcher and engraver now practising in Germany, was asked to prepare work in collaboration with a British writer, the poet Kevin Crossley-Holland, whom I commissioned to write a poem about the Ridgeway.

The final complement of some 120 works, in many media from crayon to oils, was exhibited at the Museum and Art Gallery, Swindon. From Swindon to the Vale of the White Horse or Uffington Castle is no more than a few miles, so exhibition and pathway could be visited within a single afternoon. To observe how a landscape artist adapts or moulds his subject to his own vision can provide valuable insights into both, all the more so when there is an overlap or coincidence of subject matter among a number of artists working independently.

The appeal of the Ridgeway is not easy to pinpoint. It has something to do with the unusual height of the track, where nothing separates you from the sky. There is a powerful contrast between this broad open space and the dense clumps of trees, distributed almost like sculpture at strangely satisfying intervals. Each of the artists came to his own terms with the 'presence' of this landscape. Patrick Malacarnet from Jersey saw the Uffington White Horse and some configurations of stones around Avebury with a glowing intensity bordering on the surreal. Keith Grant was attracted by the landscape of winter, as was Philip Hughes, who investigated stretches of the track on skis. Robert Collins camped out for weeks in the early spring to absorb the atmosphere which he re-created in delicate studies of fields and flowers. Paola Nero, an American painter working on a large scale, flew over the Ridgeway in a hydrogen balloon to sketch the ancient contours of the landscape, while Gordon Joy produced an extensive sequence of miniature paintings tracing complete sections of longer walks. At Barbury Castle Graham Hillier found the old track exerting such an hypnotic force that the surrounding landscape became distilled into a single numinous haze.

Assembling the Ridgeway paintings once more, as an accompaniment to Richard Ingrams' eloquent essay, has given them a new life. It is now possible to see the landscape and its interpretations simultaneously, giving to the present book a dual role: a view of some approaches to landscape painting today which is, equally, a walking companion to this magnificent stretch of classic English countryside.

London
June 1987

The Ridgeway

Richard Ingrams

> The Ridgeway carries the traveller for thirty miles as if
> along the battlements of a castle.
>
> Edward Thomas: *The Icknield Way*

'Over the hills and far away' is the most romantic line in English
poetry. It appeals especially to those of us who live in the South,
where the country, as one crosses it, whether on foot or by
car, sometimes seems to consist of row upon row of chalk
downland ranging from east to west. Beyond one line of hills
lies another line of hills, and then another, and then, perhaps,
the sea, which in our little island is never very far away.

If 'over the hills and far away' sums up our feeling of hope
that adventure lies over the horizon, so there is no more excit-
ing sight than a white chalk track winding off between fields
and hedges into the distance. It invites exploration and offers
an escape from metalled roads and cars. On many of these ridges
of downland there will be found such a path, almost invariably
on the north side of the hill and not running directly along
the top. Such paths are what R. Hippisley Cox called in the
romantic phrase with which he titled his book, 'The Green
Roads of England', ancient trackways linking up the hilltop
encampments at vantage points of the downs where the Iron
Age inhabitants of Britain lived, now empty arenas of grassland
that are bounded by huge green ramparts and grazed by sheep.

Historians guess that there was one such 'green road' running from Norfolk all the way to Devon. But the route it took

Left:
Gordon Joy. View over Bald Hill
(Icknield Way). *Acrylic, 1986*

Gordon Joy. East from Coombe
Hill (Icknield Way). *Acrylic,
1986*

is inevitably a matter of dispute. What is extraordinary, and
not a subject of speculation at all, is that in Berkshire and Wiltshire a Ridgeway of about forty miles, perhaps a part of this
longer road, has survived intact to the present day. Because
of its superior length it is known as *The* Ridgeway, sometimes
the Berkshire Ridgeway. ('The Ridgeway Path' is a name
recently given by the Countryside Commission to a route that
includes the Ridgeway and also part of the old Icknield Way
north of the Thames between Goring and Ivinghoe in Buck-
inghamshire.) The Ridgeway, we are told by those who know,
dates from about 2000 BC and so is far older than any Roman
road. It owes its survival to the fact that until the early years
of this century, when farmers began to plough and cultivate
the land there, the Berkshire Downs were used almost
exclusively for the grazing of sheep and the Ridgeway provided
an invaluable wide and grassy highway for getting them to and
from market, especially since flocks of sheep have a way of

Right:
Gordon Joy. Cornfields near
Coombe Hill (Icknield Way).
Acrylic, 1985

Gordon Joy. Looking west
towards Blewbury Down.
Acrylic, 1985

destroying surfaced roads with their hooves. East Ilsley, just
off the Ridgeway, was famous for its annual sheep fair where,
it is estimated, around 80,000 sheep would be bought and sold.

The Ridgeway was 'discovered' by Richard Jefferies in the
1870s in the same way that William Stukeley 'discovered'
Avebury — that is to say he wrote about something that had
been there for a long time but which had remained unremarked
upon. Jefferies, a nature poet who wrote in prose, was born
at Coate near Swindon in 1848 and spent the first thirty years
of his life there. In 1879, in his book *Wild Life in a Southern
County*, he wrote the first description of the Ridgeway (though
he did not name it):

'A broad green track runs for many a long, long mile across
the downs, now following the ridges, now winding past at the
foot of a grassy slope, then stretching away through cornfield
and fallow. It is distinct from the wagon-tracks which cross
it here and there, for these are local only, and if traced up, land
the wayfarer presently in a maze of fields, or end abruptly in
the rickyard of a lone farmhouse. It is distinct from the hard

Right:
Robert Collins. Woodland path,
Streatley. *Oil, 1985*

roads of modern construction which also at wide intervals cross its course, dusty and glaringly white in the sunshine. It is not a farm track: you may walk for twenty miles along it over the hills: neither is it the King's highway . . .

'The origin of the track goes back into the dimmest antiquity: there is evidence that it was a military road when the fierce Dane carried fire and slaughter inland, leaving his "nailed bark" in the creeks of the rivers, and before that when the Saxons pushed up from the sea. The eagles of old Rome, perhaps, were borne along it, and yet earlier the chariots of the Britons may have used it — traces of all have been found: so that for fifteen centuries this track of the primitive peoples has maintained its existence through the strange changes of the times, till now in the season the cumbrous steam ploughing engines jolt and strain and pant over the uneven turf . . .'

Today the walker can pick up the Ridgeway, now clearly signposted by the Countryside Commission, near the golf course at Streatley on Thames. It rises slowly through a tunnel of trees until after about a mile it comes out into the open downland above Streatley Warren where the walker can look back over the Thames valley and the Chiltern hills beyond. Past Warren Farm, the horizon widens to include the Wittenham Clumps and even, on a clear day, the distant towers of Oxford. 'A rough way,' Edward Thomas described it when he explored the Ridgeway in 1910, 'now wide, now narrow, among the hazel, brier, elder and nettle. Sometimes there was an ash in the hedge and once a line of spindly elms followed it round a curve.' (That 'line of spindly elms', which I myself knew well, has alas fallen prey to the Dutch elm disease, though to make up for them there is a fine ash tree where another track branches off to Lowbury Hill, once the site of a Roman temple and where oyster shells can still be found in the turf.)

Edward Thomas, the poet and journalist who was tragically killed in the First World War, was a disciple of Richard Jefferies, whose life he wrote. He was a great lover of England

Gordon Joy. View towards Streatley from Warren Farm. *Acrylic, 1986*

Douglas Harding. Scutchamer Knob.
Acrylic on paper, 1986

Right :
Philip Hughes. Wether Down,
looking west. *Mixed media, 1986*

Philip Hughes. Wether Down.
Mixed media, 1986

as well as a compulsive walker, who tramped his way over most
of the southern counties of England during his short life.
Writers have always been in the habit of going for long walks
— to cheer themselves up or work out their ideas — which
partly explains why the Ridgeway has such a rich and diverse
literature. But in the second half of the nineteenth century a
new generation of Romantics led by Robert Louis Stevenson
created a walking cult. Stevenson, who trekked across the
Cevennes with his donkey, appealed to the late Victorians with
his simple, if sentimental, prayer for 'the open road and the
sky above me' and his notion of travelling hopefully.

One of Stevenson's keenest followers was Kenneth Grahame, the author of *The Wind in the Willows*. Grahame was a
nature worshipper who derived his religion from the writings
of Richard Jefferies and was even, in his youth, numbered

Right:
Jonathan Briggs. The path across
the field. *Acrylic, 1985*

Malte Sartorius. Two bushes.
Etching, 1986

among a group of writers known as the New Pagans. But it
would have been hard to imagine anyone less like a pagan than
Grahame, a tall mustachioed Scotsman, quiet, reserved and
gentlemanly, who would have run a mile from a Roman orgy.
In spite of his success, his personal life was, from beginning
to end, a long catalogue of misfortune. His mother died when
he was five and his father, a drunkard, banished him and his
brothers and sister to the care of their maternal grandmother
at Cookham Dean. He was deprived of the Oxford education
he longed for and eventually made a career in the Bank of England. His marriage to Elspeth Thomson was a disaster, and their
only child Alistair was handicapped from birth by bad eyesight
and eventually committed suicide at the age of nineteen. Not

Right:
Jonathan Briggs. Cloud shadows,
looking north towards
Childrey Warren. *Acrylic, 1985*

The edge of the Long Plantation overhangs the way   *The way turns at Seven Barrows*   *Hill Barn Clump*   *Rubbishpit Plantation*

surprisingly in view of this tragic background, Grahame developed into a solitary, self-possessed dreamer who put all his complicated, very English feelings into the characters of *The Wind in the Willows*, characters like Ratty and Mole who live an idyllic bachelor life by the river, untroubled by worries and wives. All his life Grahame liked walking, and especially walking alone: 'For Nature's particular gift to the walker, through the semi-mechanical act of walking — a gift no other form of exercise seems to transmit in the same high degree — is to set the mind jogging, to make it garrulous, exalted, a little mad maybe — certainly creative and suprasensitive, until at last it really seems to be outside of you and as it were talking to you, while you are talking back to it. Then everything gradually seems to join in, sun and wind, the white road and the dusty hedges, the spirit of the season, whichever that may be, the friendly old earth that is pushing forth life of every sort under your feet or spell-bound in death-like winter trance, till you walk in the midst of a blessed company, immersed in a dream-talk far transcending any possible human conversation.'

In 1910 when he retired from the Bank of England at the age of forty-nine, Grahame and his wife moved to a thatched farmhouse called Boham's in Blewbury. He was to spend

Philip Hughes. Walk from Uffington to Sparsholt Firs. *Mixed media, 1986*

Right:
Douglas Harding. Sparsholt Down. *Acrylic on paper, 1986*

Jonathan Briggs. Wantage
Down. *Acrylic, 1985*

Gordon Joy. View from Britwell
Hill (Icknield Way). *Acrylic,
1985*

fourteen years here before moving to Pangbourne, where he
died in 1932. Grahame had loved the Berkshire downland all
his life and one of the advantages of living in Blewbury was
that he could walk up onto the Ridgeway every day and tramp
along it for miles and miles. In his first book, *Pagan Papers*
(1898), he had described in typically Stevensonian tones the pull
of the 'Rudge':

'Join it at Streatley, the point where it crosses the Thames;
at once it strikes you out and away from the habitable world
in a splendid purposeful manner, running along the highest
ridge of the Downs, a broad green ribbon of turf, with but
a shade of difference from the neighbouring grass, yet distinct
for all that. No villages nor homesteads tempt it aside or modify
its course for a yard; should you lose the track where it is blent
with the bordering turf or merged in and obliterated by criss-
cross paths you have only to walk straight on, taking heed of
no alternative to right or left; and in a minute 'tis with you

Right :
Graham Hillier. The Vale of the
White Horse. *Acrylic, 1986*

Patrick Malacarnet. White
Horse country. *Tempora, 1986*

Right:
Paola Nero. Dancing horse.
Pastel, 1986

Philip Hughes. The Manger, from White Horse Hill. *Mixed media, 1986*

again — arisen out of the earth as it were. Or, if still not quite assured, lift you your eyes, and there it runs over the brow of the fronting hill. Where a railway crosses it, it disappears indeed — hiding Alpheus-like, from the ignominy of rubble and brickwork; but a little way on it takes up the running again with the same quiet persistence. Out on that almost trackless expanse of billowy Downs such a track is in some sort humanly companionable; it really seems to lead you by the hand.'

Grahame would perhaps be less rhapsodic today. The railway which he describes (the Didcot, Newbury and Southampton line) has, ironically, been dismantled and is itself a grassy track rather like the Ridgeway. But the views of the downs at this, the eastern end, the downs that Kenneth Grahame knew, are marred by two great eyesores: the sprawling, unplanned Atomic Energy Research Establishment at Harwell and the more recent Didcot power station with its massive cooling towers rising on the plain like giant elephants' feet. Then there

Right:
Robert Collins. Poppy field east of Uffington. *Oil, 1985*

Keith Grant. Uffington White Horse. *Oil and acrylic, 1986*

is the A34, now a dual carriageway, down which thunders a nonstop stream of lorries plying backwards and forwards between the Midlands and Southampton.

It is at Gore Hill where the A34 crosses it that the Ridgeway becomes recognizably the Ridgeway and here, as the rumble of the lorries slowly dies away, that the modern walker can begin to experience something of what Edward Thomas described in *The Icknield Way* (1913).

'Hedges no longer bounded either side of the broad turf track. It was as free as the blue paths in the snowy heavens. It looked down upon everything but the clouds, and not seldom on them in the early morning or in rain. On its left the downward slope was broken and very gradual, so that it was far rarer to see a church tower like Ilsley within a mile than a ridge of woods five miles off or a bare range that might be twenty. It was already higher than the Icknield Way at Telegraph Hill: it had climbed out of choice and it would descend only of necessity. On its right the slope was far steeper, and sometimes a

Right:
Graham Hillier. Uffington Castle, early morning. *Acrylic, 1985*

little way from the foot lay the villages: sometimes the land rose again in several rolls this way and that, and the nearest village would be beyond the last of them, three or four miles away . . .

'Now the Ridgeway had risen up to its perfect freedom, away from the river and the low land, from the glaring roads and the collections of houses. This way men of old came from necessity; yet I found it hard not to think now that the road was thus climbing to heights of speculation, to places suited for exploring the ridges and solitudes of the spirit; it seemed in one mood a hermit road going out of the wilderness to meditate and be in lifelong retirement; in another mood a road for the young, eager warrior or reformer going up and away for a time from cloying companions to renew his mighty youth.'

Before the gods that made the gods
  Had seen their sunrise pass
The White Horse of the White Horse Vale
  Was cut out of the grass.

G. K. Chesterton

The White Horse of Uffington lies almost exactly halfway between Streatley and Avebury, a twenty-mile walk in either direction. Like all prehistoric survivals — Avebury, Silbury Hill, the Ridgeway itself — it cocks a snook at the historian, the expert and other professional providers of information. Nobody knows for certain what its purpose is, what it commemorates (if anything) or even who put it there. In the modern world when every secret is out and instant factual data are available for all fields of inquiry, such lack of information is reassuring. No one who walks along the Ridgeway need feel ignorant.

Keith Grant. Uffington Horse and White Horse Hill. *Oil and acrylic, 1986*

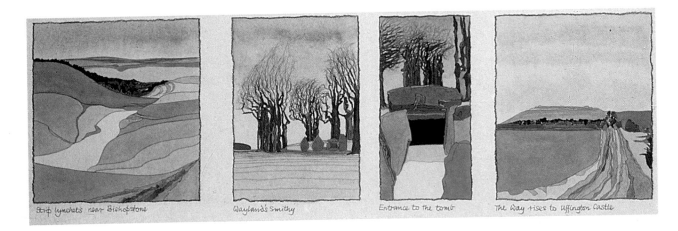

Strip lynchets near Bishopstone   Wayland's Smithy   Entrance to the tomb   The Way rises to Uffington Castle

He is just as knowledgeable as the professional archaeologist.

There is another difficulty attaching to the White Horse, namely that it is quite hard even to see it properly. Perhaps the best view is to be had from the train between Didcot and Swindon. At a distance you can see its long lean outline, drawn as if with a few bold strokes of a giant's crayon, prancing across the downs in all its ancient elegance and defying all questions about its origins, including the especially interesting one of how the ancient draughtsmen were able to create such a precise and stylish image on such a huge scale.

Paul Nash wrote in 1938: 'The White Horse is, I believe, by far the earliest hill drawing we have in England. It is a piece of design, also in another category from the rest of the great chalk figures, for it has the lineament of a work of art. The horse, which is more of a dragon than a horse, is cut on the top of the down's crest, so that it is only seen completely from the air or, at a long view, from the surrounding country. Seen on its own hill, it becomes an affair of violent foreshortenings or tapering perspectives more or less indecipherable.

'But it was precisely this aspect of the Horse design that I found so significant. Once the futile game of "picking out" the White Horse is abandoned, the documentary importance

Philip Hughes. Walk from Bishopstone to White Horse Hill. *Mixed media, 1986*

Right:
John Blandy. Over the Manger towards Dragon Hill and the White Horse. *Pastel, 1986*

1.15   8.3.86   Over the manger towards Dragons Hill & the White Horse.

Malte Sartorius. Dark landscape. *Etching, 1986*

of the site fades, and the *landscape* asserts itself with all the force of its triumphant fusion of natural and artificial design. You then perceive a landscape of terrific animation whose bleak character and stark expression accord perfectly with its lonely situation on the summit of the bare downs.'

Tradition, as opposed to the experts, always maintained that the White Horse commemorated the victory of King Alfred over the Danes at the battle of Ashdown in 870. The experts, however, insist that it is much older; and they are probably right. But tradition is not to be dismissed as if it is just a collection of fairy stories, and in the case of the White Horse common sense alone suggests that such an elaborate and magnificent monument must have been inspired by some important event. As it happens, the Ridgeway country is historically associated with two great victories over heathen invaders: Alfred's over

Right:
Graham Hillier. From Uffington, looking east at dawn. *Acrylic, 1985*

Patrick Malacarnet.
Skies of history.
Tempera, 1986

Jonathan Briggs. Fields near the Ridgeway, Farnborough Down. *Acrylic, 1985*

the Danes, and the much earlier battle of Mount Badon in about 490 at which King Arthur at the head of the Romano-British forces turned back the army of invading Saxons. In neither case can the site of the battle be precisely located, though tradition (again, for what it's worth) associates Liddington Hill with Arthur's great victory. Whatever the truth of these matters it cannot be perverse or inappropriate if we insist on regarding the White Horse of Uffington as a symbol of Christian England victorious over invading pagans.

The White Horse is linked also with that most English of all books, *Tom Brown's Schooldays*. The author Thomas Hughes (1822–96) was born and brought up in the village of Uffington which lies below the downs, and he describes the country in the first chapter of his famous book in which he rebukes his fellow Englishmen for travelling all over Europe and ignoring the beauties of their own country: 'And then what a hill is the

Right:
Jonathan Briggs. Evening sky, near Rats Hill. *Acrylic, 1985*

Douglas Harding. Fox Hill.
Acrylic on paper, 1986

White Horse Hill! There it stands right up above all the rest,
nine hundred feet above the sea, and the boldest, bravest shape
for a chalk hill that you ever saw. Let us go to the top of him
and see what is to be found there. Aye, you may well wonder
and think it odd you never heard of this before; but wonder
or not, as you please, there are hundreds of such things lying
about England which wiser folk than you know nothing of
and care nothing for . . . The ground falls rapidly on all sides.
Was there ever such turf in the whole world? You sink up to
your ankles at every step, and yet the spring of it is delicious
. . . It is altogether a place you won't forget — a place to open
a man's soul and make him prophesy, as he looks down on
that great vale spread out as the garden of the Lord before him
and wave on wave of the mysterious downs behind: and to
the right and left the chalk hills running away into the distance,

Right:
Graham Hillier. Looking east
from Liddington Castle.
Acrylic, 1985

Malte Sartorius. Sheep I.
Etching, 1986

along which he can trace the old Roman [*sic*] road, "The Ridge-way" ("the Rudge" as the country folk call it) keeping straight along the highest back of the hills.'

In a subsequent but less successful book, *The Scouring of the White Horse*, published in 1859, Hughes described the fun and games that took place two years earlier when the White Horse was cleaned for the last time by the villagers of Uffington, an event that lived on in folk memory almost as vividly as the battle of Ashdown. Scourings had been held at irregular intervals certainly since the early eighteenth century, the custom being for the villagers to climb the hill, clear away all the grass

Right:
Graham Hillier. Wayland's
Smithy from Uffington Castle.
Acrylic, 1985

Robert Collins. The Ridgeway,
early spring. *Oil, 1985*

and weeds from the chalk areas of the horse and celebrate the
event with a day or even two days of various sports and revels,
involving races of all kinds and other unusual competitions.
In 1776, for example, a waistcoat worth 10s. 6d. was offered
to the first person who could extract a bullet out of a tub of
flour. The 'scourings' caught the imagination of country people
and the various races and sporting events eventually attracted
competitors from all over the country. According to the *Reading
Mercury*, a crowd of some 30,000 people assembled in 1780 to
watch the champion-wrestling and men chasing cheeses down
the hill or trying to catch a pig. In his book Hughes vividly
pictures the scenes of 1857: Uffington Castle filled with booths
and stalls, tents and platforms, the throng of gentlemen and
ladies, gypsies and tramps. But the old country sports, and especially the backsword competitions in which brawny men set
about each other with wooden staves and frequently drew
blood, proved too savage for polite Victorian society and the
1857 scouring turned out to be the last one. Today the Horse

Right:
Philip Hughes. Strip lynchets
near Bishopstone. *Mixed media,*
1986

is the responsibility of the Department of the Environment, who carry out the necessary restoration work in a less colourful style.

Another famous and very English Englishman who lived in Uffington was the poet John Betjeman, who set up house with his young wife Penelope at Garrards Farm in 1934. Looking back many years later in a poem addressed to his one-time neighbour in the village, Stuart Piggott, he remembered

> . . . those spontaneous Berkshire days
> In straw-thatched
>   chalk built
>   pre-War
>   Uffington
> Before the March of Progress had begun
> When all the world seemed waiting to be won
> When evening air with mignonette was scented
> And picture windows had not been invented
> When shooting foxes still was thought unsporting
> And White Horse Hill was still the place for courting.

Penelope Betjeman, daughter of a field-marshal, was an intrepid horsewoman and traveller and one of the great English eccentrics. Pert, snub-nosed and very pretty, she spoke several languages and had a special interest in the art and religion of India where she was brought up. Visitors to Garrards Farm were encouraged to defecate in the kitchen garden for the good of the soil. One male guest was surprised and delighted one night to find his hostess climbing into bed with him. But it turned out that she was interested only in his spiritual welfare. 'Now tell me,' she began in her upper-class Cockney voice, 'why is it that you don't accept the divinity of Our Lord?' The love of her life was horses. She filled the Uffington cottage with saddles, bridles and other bits of tackle, and rode all over the

Graham Hillier. Barbury Castle. *Acrylic, 1986*

Patrick Malacarnet. Arthur's
Courtyard, Uffington Castle.
Tempera, 1986

Ridgeway on her white Arab mare Moti. For a time Penelope
Betjeman played the harmonium at services in the nearby village of Baulking, until she received the following devastating
letter from the vicar:

> My dear Penelope,
> I have been thinking over the question of the playing of the
> harmonium on Sunday evenings here and have reached the
> conclusion that I must now take it over myself.
>
> I am very grateful to you for doing it for so long and
> hate to have to ask you to give it up, but, to put it plainly,
> your playing has got worse and worse and the disaccord
> between harmonium and the congregation is becoming
> destructive of devotion. People are not very sensitive here,
> but even some of them have begun to complain, and they
> are not usually given to doing that. I do not like writing
> this, but I think you will understand that it is my business
> to see that divine worship is as perfect as it can be made.
> Perhaps the crankiness of the instrument has something to
> do with the trouble. I think it does require a careful and
> experienced player to deal with it.
>
> Thank you ever so much for stepping so generously into

Right:
Gordon Joy. Barbury Castle.
Acrylic, 1985

Philip Hughes. Avebury. *Mixed media, 1986*

the breach when Sibyl was ill: it was the greatest possible help to me and your results were noticeably better then than now.

Yours ever
F. P. Harton

After the war the Betjemans lived for six years in the beautiful seventeenth-century rectory of Farnborough, another Berkshire village within easy reach of the Ridgeway. There is now a window in Farnborough church designed by John Piper in memory of his great friend. It is a wonderful splash of colour at the west end of the church, celebrating the natural world of plants, butterflies and fish. In 1987 a memorial sarsen stone in memory of Penelope was set up alongside the Ridgeway, on the edge of Lockinge Estate, by her daughter Candida. The

Right:
Keith Grant. Monoliths, new moon, barn and horse. *Oil and acrylic, 1986*

Keith Grant. Sunset with standing stone. *Oil and acrylic, 1986*

Malte Sartorius. Landscape near Avebury. *Etching, 1986*

inscription, beautifully engraved by Simon Verity, reads: 'In memory of Penelope Betjeman (1910–1986) who loved the Ridgeway.'

Alongside the Ridgeway a mile or so from White Horse Hill stands the long low neolithic burial mound known as Wayland's Smithy. The tradition was that if you left your horse here overnight with a coin on one of the stones, you could return in the morning to find the coin gone and the horse shod. This impressive monument, fronted by four giant sarsen stones and surrounded by a screen of slender beech trees, is similar in design to the long barrow of West Kennett near Avebury, from which over forty bodies were recovered. A mere thirteen bodies were found in Wayland's Smithy when it was excavated in 1962–3. Three leaf-shaped arrowheads with their tips broken lay by the skeletons. The burial chamber is now dated to 2,800 BC, but the rest is speculation. Nobody knows who was buried

Right:
Paola Nero. Barbury Castle. *Oil and alkyd, 1985*

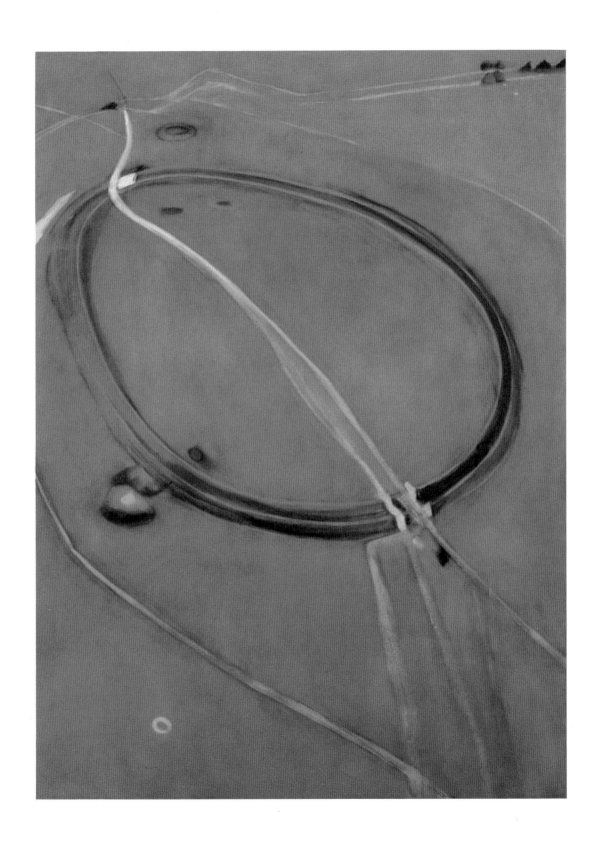

Keith Grant. Standing stones in winter. *Oil and acrylic, 1986*

here in such a magnificent tomb.

Five miles from the White Horse the Ridgeway comes down to meet Ermine Street (a Roman road) near a pub with the pleasing name of the Shepherd's Rest. From here there is a choice of routes. The old maps mark the Ridgeway running along the valley following the course of the road past the village of Chiseldon before becoming a track again and climbing up to Barbury Castle. The Countryside Commission has signposted another route which, though longer, has the advantage of less road surface, as well as being more picturesque. For a start, it takes the walker up to the top of Liddington Hill, one of the great Wiltshire landmarks, a long, low, table-topped eminence crowned with a distinctive clump of stunted windswept beech trees which now towers above the M4 as it cuts through the downs towards Swindon.

Liddington Hill is the middle in a line of three great hillforts or 'castles' which lie along the western end of the Ridgeway. It is a place sacred to the memory of Richard Jefferies, who is now commemorated on the Triangulation Point on the hill.

Right:
Anton Krajnc. Early morning at West Kennett Avenue. *Pencil and crayon on handmade paper, 1986*

Patrick Malacarnet. Near Avebury. *Tempera, 1986*

Jefferies died of tuberculosis in 1887 at the age of thirty-eight. Like many consumptives, he was a man of intense vision who responded with special acuteness to all the wonders of the natural world. But he was far from being an airy-fairy 'mystic', and in his early books, written at Coate, he describes the life and work of farm-labourers, gamekeepers and poachers, as well as the topography of the area, with great sympathy and affection. The atmosphere of the downs, the Ridgeway and the hill-forts had the profoundest effect on him and inspired some of his most lyrical writing. In his last book, *The Story of My Heart*, he tells how as a young man he would climb Liddington Hill 'to breathe a new air and to have a fresher aspiration . . .

'Moving up the sweet, short turf, at every step my heart seemed to obtain a wider horizon of feeling: with every inhalation of rich, pure air a deeper desire. The very light of the sun was whiter and more brilliant here. By the time I had reached the summit I had entirely forgotten the petty circumstances and the annoyances of existence. I felt myself, myself. There was an intrenchment on the summit, and going down into the fosse,

Right:
Anton Krajnc. Rainbow—the Ridgeway. *Pencil and crayon on handmade paper, 1986*

John Blandy. East Kennett
Barrow from the Ridgeway.
Pastel, 1985

I walked round it slowly to recover breath. On the south-
western side there was a spot where the outer bank had partially
slipped, leaving a gap. There the view was over a broad plain,
beautiful with wheat, and inclosed by a perfect amphi-theatre
of green hills. Through these hills there was one narrow
groove, or pass, southwards where the white clouds seemed
to close in the horizon. Woods hid the scattered hamlets and
farmhouses, so that I was quite alone. I was utterly alone with
the sun and earth. Lying down on the grass, I spoke in my
soul to the earth, the sun, the air and the distant sea far beyond
sight.'

   'Jefferies often thought of the sea upon these hills,' wrote
Edward Thomas in his life of the great naturalist. 'The eye
sometimes expects it. There is something oceanic in their
magnitude, their ease, their solitude — above all in their liquid
forms, that combine apparent mobility with placidity, and in
the vast playground which they provide for the shadows of
the clouds. They are never abrupt, but flowing on and on, make

Right:
Graham Hillier. Standing
stones, Avebury. *Acrylic, 1985*

a type of infinity. A troop, a clump, or a sprinkling of trees, a little wood, a house, squares of wheat or newly ploughed land cannot detract from them — not even when the air is so clear that all sounds and sights and smells are bright and have a barb that plants them deep, and the hard black rooks slide in crystal under the blue.'

When Thomas walked the Ridgeway he followed the road that passes south of Chiseldon and then the track up to Barbury Castle, last of the great hillforts with a massive double ditch and wonderful views of the surrounding downland. Regrettably, environmental bureaucrats have chosen to create something here called the Barbury Country Park, which is signposted on the Swindon–Marlborough road and which is nothing much more than a massive car park to the east of the castle, complete with information centre and unpleasant lavatories. Here in this gigantic litter trap the tourist may learn from fading fact-sheets about the life of Richard Jefferies, a man who more than anyone would have abominated the whole idea of organized 'leisure'.

The final few miles to Avebury are undoubtedly the finest. The Wiltshire countryside is open and unspoiled and the Ridgeway now broadens out and becomes a green road, while another line of downs opens up across the valley of the Kennet; and all around are those distinctive dark clumps of beech trees which are peculiar to this part of the world. As the track nears its end there are too, on the verges, huge sarsen stones (or 'Grey Wethers') which signal the approach to Avebury. Eventually the Ridgeway reaches the Bath Road (A4), where it abruptly ends. But it can be picked up on the far side of the village of East Kennett and continues up till it meets the Wansdyke, one of the many wonders of Wiltshire, and finally peters out above the Vale of Pewsey. The wise traveller will turn off before he reaches the Bath Road and walk down into Avebury, as there could be no more fitting place to end a journey. From the Ridgeway, not much can be seen except the outline of a village

Philip Hughes. Avebury. *Mixed media, 1986*

Malte Sartorius. Sheep II.
Etching, 1986

the deep waterlogged ruts deter motorists from driving down the Ridgeway. This, despite vociferous campaigns to ban all vehicles, they are perfectly within their rights to do. Nor does the mud do anything to keep away huge roaring motorcycles whose riders treat the Ridgeway as a wonderful forty-mile long scramble track. The downland solitude in which Richard Jefferies and Edward Thomas found their inspiration has become elusive. If this book does anything to forward the day when something is done to protect the Ridgeway from gradual destruction, then it will have served a useful purpose. Until then one can still be grateful for the fact that the Ridgeway has survived for nearly four thousand years, even if its days may now be numbered.

Aldworth
June 1987

Right:
Patrick Malacarnet. The roofless past. *Tempera, 1986*

Above the Spring Line
in celebration of the Ridgeway

Kevin Crossley-Holland

Under the moon's pale razor
under the warm eye
under the chamber of clouds
under rain-dance and hail-bounce

in this latitude of shadows

blazing the green limbs
foot-friend and far-reacher
master of compounds

Overseer of Epona and the fleet horses at Lambourn
the bigwigs in their hill-stations at Silbury and Chequers

keeper of Dragon Hill and the craters on the bombing range
also the quaking grass the brome grass meliot and eyebright

warden of the Og and the watercress beds and Goring Gap
the sarsens like dowdy sheep and the dowdy sheep like sarsens

custodian of the downs and brakes the strip lynchets and warrens
under the lapwing the glider's wing spring of yellow-hammers

And spring is the word. I can almost forget
yesterday — the sweat stain semen stain smudge
of chalk and in the hedge the sodden butts
the jagged bottle and a bloodstained rag

Here are wiry snowdrops bedded in beech mast
where wild pigs rooted. Fuses everywhere
The spindle and bryony shrug their shoulders
Birch-twigs pinken, generations within

A man laps at a dewpond, lays his hoar-head on his knapsack
knobby with Brandon flint. A girl in a mauve shift bares her throat
Trials riders tight-lipped burn through crimson and purple rosettes

A crocodile of the literal-minded steamy and singing
I will lift up mine eyes set their sights on the escarpment

Ah! the drover sleeps in a butterfly wimple — chalk-hill blues
flutter in and out of his mouth and here above the spring line
a hunter smiles as he snares such a pretty Chiltern gentian

It is all within me
written in chalk, and written
in your hand it is yours

whatever you may also choose . . .

From Overton to Ivinghoe
sunlight and ribs of shadows
pressing behind us and coursing
through us. We are conductors

The Artists

John Blandy (b. 1951, Suffolk) studied at Norwich School of Art, St Martin's School of Art and the Royal College of Art, London. He has exhibited widely in England since 1973. Pastel is the medium he favours, sometimes expanding studies into larger paintings in other media.

Jonathan Briggs (b. 1956, Sheffield) has worked briefly in the archaeology department of the Sheffield City Museums. He has shown works on three occasions at the Graves Art Gallery, Sheffield, including 'A Portrait of Sheffield' exhibition (1978).

Robert Collins (b. 1952, Gloucester) trained at Gloucester College of Art and the Royal College of Art, London. Between 1978 and 1982 he was active as an art therapist. Based now on the south coast, Collins specializes in painting landscapes and interiors, often with figures. He works mainly in oils and acrylic.

Keith Grant (b. 1930, Liverpool) trained at the Royal College of Art. Since 1959 he has held over twenty one-man exhibitions in England, Iceland, Italy and Norway. His work is in public collections in England, Canada, Scandinavia and Australia. Major public commissions have included mosaic murals for Newcastle upon Tyne subway. In 1986 and 1987 Grant travelled to the northernmost regions of Norway and his 'Paintings of the Frozen North' formed his second one-man exhibition at the Francis Kyle Gallery (1987).

Douglas Harding (b. 1941, Surrey) studied architecture at Kingston Polytechnic. In 1970 he moved to Paris and began to paint without any formal training. In the years he has lived in Paris, Harding has regularly travelled in the French provinces, and in 1978 he spent a year on the move in the United States.

Harding has participated in public exhibitions in Paris and Rouen, and he has held two exhibitions at the Francis Kyle Gallery (1981 and 1985).

Graham Hillier was born in Bridlington in 1946. Since 1974 he has held six one-man exhibitions of paintings and drawings besides participating in numerous group exhibitions. His response to the Ridgeway project was as a painter with a special fondness for woodland and traces of ancient history. In autumn 1986 Hillier participated in a theme exhibition at the Francis Kyle Gallery entitled 'The Lost Domain', which was devoted to the landscape of Alain-Fournier's childhood; in 1987 he held his first one-man exhibition of paintings at the gallery.

Philip Hughes (b. 1936, London) has been painting since the mid-1960s, mostly drawing his subject matter from visits he has regularly made to the remote and sacred places of the world; these range from the Inca citadel of Machu Picchu to the stone circles of Callanish in the Outer Hebrides. His paintings are regularly exhibited in France and between 1979 and 1987 he held four one-man exhibitions at the Francis Kyle Gallery.

Gordon Joy (b. 1948, Doncaster) was inspired to become a painter by school visits to the Lake District. His art-school training in the 1960s inclined him towards Pop Art, but he has since decided to revive his earlier ambitions in landscape. The success of his landscape paintings at a show in Tokyo was instrumental in encouraging him to take part in the Ridgeway project.

Anton Krajnc (b. 1949, Graz) studied at the Vienna Academy of Fine Arts and the Academia Raffaello in Urbino. He has held twenty-one one-man exhibitions in Austria, Germany, Italy, Japan, Great Britain and the United States, and he has received major graphics awards from French, Austrian and American institutions. He is represented in international collections — the Albertina, Vienna, the Chicago Art Institute and the Brooklyn Museum, New York.

Since 1973 Krajnc has divided his time between Long Island, New York, and various favourite locations near Salzburg. He has also travelled to the remoter centres of ancient civilizations, from the Nile valley to the Li river in southern mainland China.

Krajnc's works for the Ridgeway project are in pencil and crayon on his own hand-made paper which embodies a 'White Horse' watermark created for this occasion.

Patrick Malacarnet was born in Paris in 1958 and after an early childhood divided between Paris and Provence moved to Jersey where he completed his education and worked for a period as a journalist on a local paper. After a brief period of National Service in the French army he returned to the Channel Islands as a working base for his career as an artist. Malacarnet's regular travels have included trips to the United States, Africa and the Middle East.

Paola Nero (b. 1951, Rhode Island) trained at the Rhode Island School of Design. She subsequently studied in Rome and San Francisco and held exhibitions in Paris and in Rome on three occasions (1980–1). She participated in the Ridgeway project in late autumn 1985, characteristically working from a hydrogen balloon.

Malte Sartorius (b. 1933, East Prussia) studied in Göttingen and Stuttgart. Now based for much of the year in southern Spain, he is widely recognized as one of Germany's senior etchers and has participated in over two hundred group exhibitions in Europe and North America. Since 1959 he has held fifty one-man exhibitions in West Germany, Spain, Holland and France. He exhibited at the Barbican Gallery in London in 1983 and has held two exhibitions at the Francis Kyle Gallery (1984 and 1986).

Jean-Marie Toulgouat (b. 1927, Giverny, Eure) is a grandson of Impressionist painter Theodore Butler. After attending the Nice Academy of Painting, Toulgouat studied architecture at Vernon; in 1950 he went to Paris, where he practised for sixteen years before returning to Giverny.

Toulgouat's principal subject is landscape, mostly either Provence or Giverny and its neighbourhood. He has had nine one-man exhibitions in France, Holland and the United States, and had his first British exhibition in London in 1985. In that year he visited Wiltshire for the Ridgeway project to paint his first works in England. In 1987 he held his second one-man exhibition of paintings at the Francis Kyle Gallery.

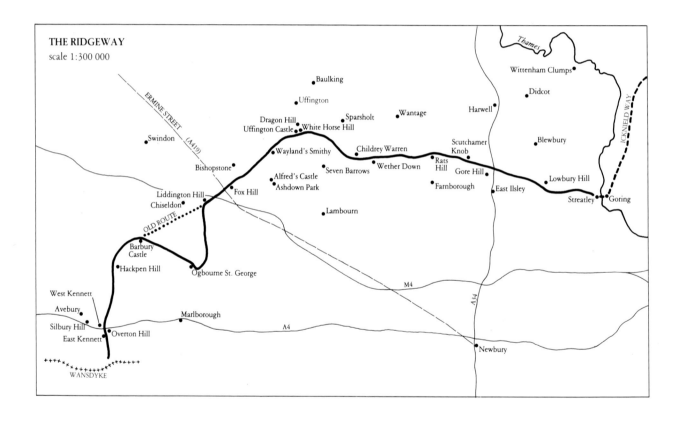

THE RIDGEWAY
scale 1:300 000

Select Bibliography

J.R.L. Anderson (with photographs by Fay Godwin): *The Oldest Road*, Wildwood, 1975

Aubrey Burl: *Prehistoric Avebury*, Yale University Press, 1979

R. Hippisley Cox: *The Green Roads of England*, 1914

Kenneth Grahame: *Pagan Papers*, 1894

Peter Green: *Kenneth Grahame, 1859–1932*, John Murray, 1959

Thomas Hughes: *The Scouring of the White Horse*, 1859

Thomas Hughes: *Tom Brown's Schooldays*, 1857

Richard Jefferies: *Jefferies' Land: History of Swindon and its Environs*, 1896

Richard Jefferies: *The Story of My Heart*, 1883

Richard Jefferies: *Wild Life in a Southern County*, 1879

Paul Nash: *Outline*, 1949

Edward Thomas: *The Icknield Way*, 1913

H.W. Timperley and Edith Brill: *Ancient Trackways of Wessex*, Dent, 1965

J.E. Vincent: *Highways and Byeways in Berkshire*, 1906

Alfred Williams: *Villages of the White Horse*, 1913

The poem on page 50 is reproduced from Bevis Hillier: *John Betjeman: A Life in Pictures*, John Murray, 1984.

Index

Driffield Hampton LECHLADE Kelmscot Radcot Hinton Waldrist

Whelford Inglesham Buscot Eaton Hastings Buckland

Marston Meysey Kempsford 278 264 Littleworth 347 Pusey Ho.

Severn 289 Down Ampney 244 Upper Inglesham 443 Wadley Ho. Pusey Charn

th Cerney Latton 259 Eisey Castle Eaton River Coleshill FARINGDON Lyt 211

River Ashton Keynes or 264 530A Hatford Wi H

Leigh 358 CRICKLADE Hannington 327 260 Coxwell Shellingford Stanford in the Vale 230

280 Purton Stoke 297 Broad Blunsdon 300 HIGHWORTH 433 Fernham Longcot 333 Balking

GLOUCESTER BR. 484 Sevenhampton 427 Watchfield 257

272 Stanton Fitzwarren G.W.Ry. VALE OF Goosey

350 Blunsdon St Andrew South Marston Shrivenham 288 Woolstone 407 Uffington Sparsholt

289 Upper Stratton Stratton St Mard 296 Compton Beauchamp Whitehorse Hill 856 Kingston Lisle 674 Childr 469

Purton Rodbourne Cheney Bourton 478 Ashbury Kingston Warren 172

Lydiard Millicent 465 Lydiard Park 308 328 Bishopstone Idstone 415 Ridge Way ICKNIELD WAY

416 Lydiard Tregoze 371 Rushey Platt Sta. SWINDON Little Hinton Ashdown Park 482 Lambourn Downs

WOOTTON BASSETT 352 417 Coate Wanborough 549 620 Upper Lambourn

267 Berks Canal Elcombe 397 Wroughton Liddington 731 538 421 LAMBOURN

Tockenham 318 Overtown Chiseldon 542 Badbury 769 Baydon Eastbury East Gar

376 Bushton 661 Uffcott 543 Draycot Foliat 551 639

Cliffe Pypard 688 Broad Town Broad Hinton 560 Upper Upham 423 Aldbourne 719

Clevancy 562 810 Woodsend 624 Stock Lane Inholmes Poughley 544

Highway 600 Winterbourne Bassett 881 Ogbourne St George Ramsbury 361 Chilton Foliat Wie

Compton Bassett Berwick Bassett Hackpen Hill 887 Marlborough Downs 635 The Manor Chilton Lodge 469 Clap

Yatesbury Winterbourne Monkton Rockley 470 Ogbourne St Andrew Littlecote 320 HUNGERFO

Avebury 512 425 Manton Ho. Arford Froxfield 360 Hund
fd Park

Cherhill 614 Beckhampton 616 559 Fyfield 444 Mildenhall 609 548 Manton 428 READING Little Bedwyn Bagshot Walkington

one Wellington 491 Wt Overton MARLBOROUGH 636 WAY 396 Inkpen

Down 523 E. Kennett 634 Savernake Cadley 547 Chisbury 400 Shalbourne

s Hill Ridge Savernake Forest Great Bedwyn 545 Ham

Mansdyke 958 St Ann's Hill 754 Savernake Ho. Walbury Hill

Bishop's Cannings 402 500 Summer Down 720 Huish Wootton Rivers Canal WESTERN 469

Horton Stanton St Bernard Alton Priors 440 Stowell Oare RAIL 596 Wilton Wood

All Cannings Avon GREAT 528 Burbage 1592 459 Buttermere

Kennet Woodborough Wilcot PEWSEY Easton Royal Grafton 700